CHANGE

CHANGE

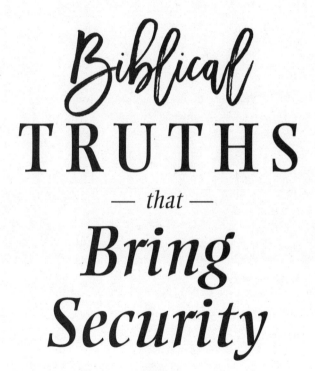

Biblical

TRUTHS

— *that* —

Bring Security

PUBLISHING GROUP

NASHVILLE, TENNESSEE

978-1-5359-1778-0

Published by B&H Publishing Group
Nashville, Tennessee

Dewey Decimal Classification: 242.5
Subject Heading: DEVOTIONAL LITERATURE \
BIBLE—INSPIRATION \ MEDITATIONS \ PRAYERS

All Scripture quotations are taken from the Christian Standard
Bible®, Copyright © 2017 by Holman Bible Publishers. Used
by permission. Christian Standard Bible® and CSB® are
federally registered trademarks of Holman Bible Publishers.

1 2 3 4 5 6 7 8 • 22 21 20 19 18

CONTENTS

CONTENTS

Somewhere along the line, the Bible attracted a reputation for being both irrelevant and impossible to understand. Out of touch as well as out of reach. Yet while conclusions like these continue to persist, so does the human need for the Bible to be everything God affirms it to be: "living and effective" (Hebrews 4:12), its message "very near you, in your mouth and in your heart" (Deuteronomy 30:14).

If families and friends are to live together in unity . . . if lives are to be whole and fruitful in heart and mind . . . if tragedy and loss and disappointment and confusion are to be survived . . . no, not merely survived but transformed into peace and power and a purposeful way forward . . . you need a Word that is here and now and able to be grasped. You need to "know the truth," because "the truth will set you free" (John 8:32).

That's why you picked up this book. As the changes in your life become overwhelming, you need to take a step back and soak in God's Word.

Filled with Scriptures that speak personally to you, this little book is further proof that God intends His Word to share living space with your present reality. Always in touch. Always within reach. No matter where you are, or what you are going through, allow this book to help direct you to the Scriptures you need most.

Sometimes it can feel like the entire world is against us. Everything is going wrong, and we are trapped in our circumstances. We become overwhelmed by the stress of the circumstances or the idea of the future. But stress is not the end. God is for us; and if that is true, who can be against us? Our eternal reassurance in the face of conflict, rejection, worry, and stress is that God's love for us is constant. No matter what kind of change you find yourself in, let these verses reassure you of the One who is always on your side.

But the LORD *said to Samuel, "Do not look at his appearance or his stature because I have rejected him. Humans do not see what the* LORD *sees, for humans see what is visible, but the* LORD *sees the heart."*

　　1 Samuel 16:7

———

"Everyone the Father gives me will come to me, and the one who comes to me I will never cast out."

　　John 6:37

But God proves his own love for us in that while we were still sinners, Christ died for us.
    Romans 5:8

———

If God is for us, who is against us?
    Romans 8:31

———

Peter began to speak: "Now I truly understand that God doesn't show favoritism, but in every nation the person who fears him and does what is right is acceptable to him."
    Acts 10:34–35

Father, I am overwhelmed with stress from the changes that are occurring in my life. I am at the point where I feel trapped in doubt and despair. Thank You for Your constant presence through the valley and for Your acceptance of me into Your family. Turn on the light so that I can find my way out of this place of despair. Continue to hold me in Your arms and never let me go. Amen

ANGER

Anger at yourself, anger at the world, anger at God; there are countless occasions for anger to rear its ugly head, and often times it comes as our first reaction to change. It's an emotion that we all feel and tend to feel the most often towards those we care about the most. The key is not to act out in anger, but to discover the root of your anger and work through the grief that is left when your anger subsides. When you are overwhelmed, never let anger be in the driver's seat, it will only lead you deeper into chaos.

Refrain from anger and give up your rage; do not be agitated—it can only bring harm.
> *Psalm 37:8*

———

A patient person shows great understanding, but a quick-tempered one promotes foolishness.
> *Proverbs 14:29*

———

A gentle answer turns away anger, but a harsh word stirs up wrath.
> *Proverbs 15:1*

"But I tell you, everyone who is angry with his brother or sister will be subject to judgment. Whoever insults his brother or sister, will be subject to the court. Whoever says, 'You fool!' will be subject to hellfire."

Matthew 5:22

———

Be angry and do not sin. Don't let the sun go down on your anger, and don't give the devil an opportunity.

Ephesians 4:26–27

Lord, right now I am holding onto anger in my heart. Wipe this anger out of me. Give me the peace and patience that I need to forgive. Remind me daily of the forgiveness that You have given me. I'm afraid that if I let go of my anger I will not have anything left. I desire to love well, but I know I cannot do this without Your guiding hand. Grant me the wisdom to know how to handle this situation in love, and to know that letting go of my anger will not leave me empty, but give room for You to fill. Amen

Anxiety can come up in every part of our lives. Beneath our anxieties is a need to feel in control. Control is impossible, and trying to hold on to it will only leave you scrambling and stressed, and ill-prepared when the unexpected change does occur. Our peace is found in knowing that the Creator of the universe holds us safely in the palm of His hand and will protect us no matter the situation in which we land. Release control to God, and allow yourself to be free in His hand.

"Therefore I tell you: Don't worry about your life, what you will eat or what you will drink; or about your body, what you will wear. Isn't life more than food and the body more than clothing? Consider the birds of the sky: They don't sow or reap or gather into barns, yet your heavenly Father feeds them. Aren't you worth more than they? Can any of you add one moment to his life-span by worrying?"

Matthew 6:25–27

————

Humble yourselves, therefore, under the mighty hand of God, so that he may exalt you at the proper time, casting all your cares on him, because he cares about you.

1 Peter 5:6–7

"Peace I leave with you. My peace I give to you. I do not give to you as the world gives. Don't let your heart be troubled or fearful."

    John 14:27

———

Don't worry about anything, but in everything, through prayer and petition with thanksgiving, present your requests to God. And the peace of God, which surpasses all understanding, will guard your hearts and minds in Christ Jesus.

    Philippians 4:6–7

———

For God has not given us a spirit of fear, but one of power, love, and sound judgment.

    2 Timothy 1:7

Heavenly Father, no matter how much I wish it was not true, there are things that are outside of my control. I worry that I am not doing enough, or too much, or am not fully known or fully loved. I feel lost without some kind of control. Help me to leave my anxieties at Your feet. I entrust to You my anxieties, knowing that Your peace will guard my heart and mind. Amen

No matter when you came to faith, whether as a small child or very late in life, you are a coheir with Christ and sealed by His Holy Spirit. There is nothing that can take you away from God's hand once you have given yourself to Him. No matter what change is happening in your life, hold firm to the promise that His grip on you will never change.

*If you confess with your mouth, "Jesus is Lord,"
and believe in your heart that God raised him from
the dead, you will be saved. One believes with the
heart, resulting in righteousness, and one confesses
with the mouth, resulting in salvation.*

    Romans 10:9–10

———

*You did not receive a spirit of slavery to fall
back into fear. Instead, you received the Spirit of
adoption, by whom we cry out, "Abba, Father!" The
Spirit himself testifies together with our spirit that
we are God's children, and if children, also heirs—
heirs of God and coheirs with Christ—if indeed
we suffer with him so that we may also be glorified
with him.*

    Romans 8:15–17

"Truly I tell you, anyone who hears my word and believes him who sent me has eternal life and will not come under judgment but has passed from death to life."

John 5:24

———

I have written these things to you who believe in the name of the Son of God so that you may know that you have eternal life.

1 John 5:13

Thank You, Lord Jesus, that I can draw near to You, for You are faithful. I know that I am sinful, and still being sanctified daily, but You will never give up on me. I am in Your hand, and by Your side for all eternity. Thank You for this assurance, Father. Thank You for never giving up on me. Amen

In the midst of change it feels impossible to remember the blessings that God has placed in our lives. But even in the unexpected, He is there. We can experience deep joy when we take notice of the abundant blessings in our lives and praise and thank the Lord for such bountiful grace, even in the midst of feeling overwhelmed. While running around, remember the provisions that God has given You.

"May the LORD bless you and protect you; may the LORD make his face shine on you and be gracious to you; may the LORD look with favor on you and give you peace."

Numbers 6:24–26

———

Indeed, we have all received grace upon grace from his fullness, for the law was given through Moses; grace and truth came through Jesus Christ.

John 1:16–17

———

And my God will supply all your needs according to his riches in glory in Christ Jesus.

Philippians 4:19

And God is able to make every grace overflow to you, so that in every way, always having everything you need, you may excel in every good work.

    2 Corinthians 9:8

———

Blessed is the God and Father of our Lord Jesus Christ, who has blessed us with every spiritual blessing in the heavens in Christ.

    Ephesians 1:3

Heavenly Father, I thank You and praise You for all the ways You have shown me mercy and grace, and I ask for the blessing of Your presence throughout this day. I know that I could not get through this time of change without Your outpouring of grace. Give me reminders today of Your goodness. Amen

Change is frightening. Whether you are mourning the loss of a loved one, preparing to leave a home you love, searching for a job, or even just finding yourself in a new stage of life, change can bring about high levels of stress. No matter what that change is, the presence of God goes before you preparing the way. Have confidence that on the other side of this change, no matter what the new world looks like, God will be there.

There is an occasion for everything, and a time for every activity under heaven.

> *Ecclesiastes 3:1*

———

"Do not remember the past events, pay no attention to things of old. Look, I am about to do something new; even now it is coming. Do you not see it? Indeed, I will make a way in the wilderness, rivers in the desert."

> *Isaiah 43:18–19*

"Because I, the LORD, have not changed, you descendants of Jacob have not been destroyed."
     Malachi 3:6

———

Therefore, if anyone is in Christ, he is a new creation; the old has passed away, and see, the new has come!
     2 Corinthians 5:17

———

Jesus Christ is the same yesterday, today, and forever.
     Hebrews 13:8

Lord Jesus, I do not know what the future holds for me, and it fills me with fear. I know that this stress is not the end of my story, and that You have a far greater plan ahead of me, but right now it is impossible for me to see. No matter what the future brings, may I take heart that You are with me until the end of the age. Bring me peace in the midst of this change, that I may not fear what is to come. Amen

None of us are immune from hardships, loss, and change, but we can take heart that no matter what has happened, the Lord promises to comfort us. Sometimes He comforts us directly; sometimes through circumstances, and sometimes through the people He places in our lives. Think about the ways that God has comforted you in your times of need.

Even when I go through the darkest valley, I fear no danger, for you are with me; your rod and your staff—they comfort me.

   Psalm 23:4

———

Remember your word to your servant; you have given me hope through it. This is my comfort in my affliction: Your promise has given me life.

   Psalm 119:49–50

———

As a mother comforts her son, so I will comfort you, and you will be comforted in Jerusalem.

   Isaiah 66:13

"Blessed are those who mourn, for they will be comforted."

Matthew 5:4

———

Blessed be the God and Father of our Lord Jesus Christ, the Father of mercies and the God of all comfort. He comforts us in all our affliction, so that we may be able to comfort those who are in any kind of affliction, through the comfort we ourselves receive from God.

2 Corinthians 1:3–4

Dear God, thank You for comforting me and healing my heart in times of trial. I am distracted by the changes going on in my life and I know that the only way out is with Your comforting hand. Thank You for putting people in my life who bring me comfort. Guide me to those whom You have chosen for me as kindred spirits. Guide my actions that I may be a source of comfort for others. Use my life as a blessing for others. Amen

When we find ourselves in the unknown, it can begin to eat away at our confidence. We allow ourselves to believe the lie that our worth is based upon what we can get done, and how in control we are. Remember that, no matter what challenges you may face, the power that created the universe and raised Christ from the dead lives inside of you. You have a greater power living inside of you than just your own ability to multi-task. You have the Holy Spirit.

"Do not fear, for I am with you; do not be afraid, for I am your God. I will strengthen you; I will help you; I will hold on to you with my righteous right hand."

    Isaiah 41:10

———

It is not that we are competent in ourselves to claim anything as coming from ourselves, but our adequacy is from God.

    2 Corinthians 3:5

———

I am able to do all things through him who strengthens me.

    Philippians 4:13

So don't throw away your confidence, which has a great reward. For you need endurance, so that after you have done God's will, you may receive what was promised.

Hebrews 10:35–36

———

This is how we will know that we belong to the truth and will reassure our hearts before him whenever our hearts condemn us; for God is greater than our hearts, and he knows all things. Dear friends, if our hearts don't condemn us, we have confidence before God and receive whatever we ask from him because we keep his commands and do what is pleasing in his sight.

1 John 3:19–22

Heavenly Father, everything is changing and I need Your help. I feel afraid and hesitant, but I know that with Your power I have no reason to feel this way. Grant me the kind of inner strength and confidence that only comes from trusting in Your love and provision for all my needs. Amen

At home, at work, in friendships, in families, in life—contentment is hard! We are constantly looking around to see what could be better, what we are missing out on or what we used to have. The quickest route to contentment is through gratitude and trust; gratitude to God for what He has provided you, and trust that He will continue to give you everything you need. Recognize the goodness in your life. See the good, and trust that God never fails to provide for your needs.

*"So don't worry, saying, 'What will we eat?' or
'What will we drink?' or 'What will we wear?'
For the Gentiles eagerly seek all these things,
and your heavenly Father knows that you need
them. But seek first the kingdom of God and his
righteousness, and all these things will be provided
for you. Therefore don't worry about tomorrow,
because tomorrow will worry about itself. Each day
has enough trouble of its own."*

Matthew 6:31–34

———

*But godliness with contentment is great gain. For
we brought nothing into the world, and we can take
nothing out. If we have food and clothing, we will
be content with these.*

1 Timothy 6:6–8

I don't say this out of need, for I have learned to be content in whatever circumstances I find myself. I know both how to make do with little, and I know how to make do with a lot. In any and all circumstances I have learned the secret of being content—whether well fed or hungry, whether in abundance or in need.

Philippians 4:11–12

———

Keep your life free from the love of money. Be satisfied with what you have, for he himself has said, I will never leave you or abandon you.

Hebrews 13:5

Heavenly Father, thank You for Your unfailing love and faithfulness. Father, when I am lost in discontentment, push me to see all that You have provided for me. Do not allow me to continue to be blind, but open my eyes to the goodness that surrounds me exactly where I am. Grow in me a godly contentment, never wishing I was anywhere but exactly where You have placed me. Amen

Sometimes the right and wrong answers are easy to see. Should I kill someone? No. Should I read my Bible? Yes. But other times the answers are not as clear. Should I move to a new place? Should I get married? How many children should I have? Which church should I join? Luckily, these are not decisions you have to make on your own. The Holy Spirit is our ever-present Helper who grants us wisdom so that we can know and do the will of God in all situations.

So give your servant a receptive heart to judge your people and to discern between good and evil. For who is able to judge this great people of yours?

   1 Kings 3:9

———

And I pray this: that your love will keep on growing in knowledge and every kind of discernment, so that you may approve the things that are superior and may be pure and blameless in the day of Christ.

   Philippians 1:9–10

———

Don't stifle the Spirit. Don't despise prophecies, but test all things. Hold on to what is good. Stay away from every kind of evil.

   1 Thessalonians 5:19–22

Now if any of you lacks wisdom, he should
ask God—who gives to all generously and
ungrudgingly—and it will be given to him.
    James 1:5

———

Dear friends, do not believe every spirit, but test the
spirits to see if they are from God, because many
false prophets have gone out into the world.
    1 John 4:1

Holy Spirit, may my spirit be open and receptive to Your prompting and leading so that I discern what is right and good in all things. Let my discernment be so strong that I can hear You calling out the directions long before I am led astray. Place in me a heart that sees truth. Amen

God places people in our lives for a reason and for our good. Seek out those who bring you encouragement. Pray for those you can encourage. Never hold in kindness that can be spread to lift up those around you. Even when you are stressed beyond measure, look for opportunities in life to cheer others up. You never know when those words are God pouring out encouragement through you to others.

The LORD is the one who will go before you. He will be with you; he will not leave you or abandon you. Do not be afraid or discouraged.

   Deuteronomy 31:8

———

God is our refuge and strength, a helper who is always found in times of trouble.

   Psalm 46:1

———

"Aren't five sparrows sold for two pennies? Yet not one of them is forgotten in God's sight. Indeed, the hairs of your head are all counted. Don't be afraid; you are worth more than many sparrows."

   Luke 12:6–7

"I have told you these things so that in me you may have peace. You will have suffering in this world. Be courageous! I have conquered the world."

John 16:33

———

And let us watch out for one another to provoke love and good works, not neglecting to gather together, as some are in the habit of doing, but encouraging each other, and all the more as you see the day approaching.

Hebrews 10:24–25

Christ Jesus, may Your Spirit strengthen and encourage my heart today. Comfort me in my grief, and lift me out of my discouraged state. Show me those around me who need my encouragement. Place on my heart those friends who need a kind word today. Allow me to be the tool You use to help lift up everyone I meet today. Amen

The tragic relativity of time is the speed with which an hour of joy passes and the lifetime a moment of despair takes, but the truth is that our entire lives are but a mark on the time line of eternity. God is outside, above, and in control of all time. While it may seem like everything is changing, the one constant we can always depend on is God, and soon enough we will be with Him for all eternity.

Before the mountains were born, before you gave birth to the earth and the world, from eternity to eternity, you are God.

   Psalm 90:2

———

He has made everything appropriate in its time. He has also put eternity in their hearts, but no one can discover the work God has done from beginning to end.

   Ecclesiastes 3:11

———

For the wages of sin is death, but the gift of God is eternal life in Christ Jesus our Lord.

   Romans 6:23

"Truly I tell you, anyone who hears my word and believes him who sent me has eternal life and will not come under judgment but has passed from death to life."

    John 5:24

———

This is eternal life: that they may know you, the only true God, and the one you have sent—Jesus Christ.

    John 17:3

Father, I know that this life is only temporary, and soon I will be with You in heaven, but that does not make the pain of today feel any less real. God, take this pain away from me. Help me to see time through Your eyes. Grant me the patience to get through this season, and the wisdom to see Your plan. Give me a vision of heaven that brings me joy in knowing that I will get to spend all eternity there with You. Amen

Failure is part of life. It is not the failure in itself, but our ability to turn around and use that failure to show our true character. Unfortunately, it is too common for us to let our failures run our lives, to create unneeded stress remembering what happened last time. Though failures of any kind can crush our spirits, we have the assurance that God's purposes can never be thwarted. Walk in victory, knowing that any past failures are in the past, and God will use all to His glory.

Now we have this treasure in clay jars, so that this extraordinary power may be from God and not from us. We are afflicted in every way but not crushed; we are perplexed but not in despair; we are persecuted but not abandoned; we are struck down but not destroyed.

  2 Corinthians 4:7–9

———

He brought me up from a desolate pit, out of the muddy clay, and set my feet on a rock, making my steps secure. He put a new song in my mouth, a hymn of praise to our God. Many will see and fear, and they will trust in the LORD.

  Psalm 40:2–3

*A person's steps are established by the L*ORD*, and he*
takes pleasure in his way. Though he falls, he will
*not be overwhelmed, because the L*ORD *supports*
him with his hand.

    Psalm 37:23–24

———

And not only that, but we also rejoice in our
afflictions, because we know that affliction
produces endurance, endurance produces proven
character, and proven character produces hope.

    Romans 5:3–4

Heavenly Father, grant me grace in times of failure and help me press forward as I fix my eyes on Jesus. Clear the failures from my mind, and do not allow them to cause me stress when I find myself in a similar situation. Thank You for the abundance of forgiveness You have poured over me. Help me to charge into this time of change with no fear of failure, knowing that whatever happens will be Your will. Amen

Families come in all shapes and sizes. They bring out our best and our worst. They are filled with bonds that can never be broken and heartache from deeply rooted hurts. The family was created by God, and He has given us some guidelines to help us flourish, to honor one another, and to push each other into Christ's arms.

*This is why a man leaves his father and mother and
bonds with his wife, and they become one flesh.*
    Genesis 2:24

———

*Honor your father and your mother so that you may
have a long life in the land that the* LORD *your God
is giving you.*
    Exodus 20:12

———

Sons are indeed a heritage from the LORD*, offspring,
a reward. . . . Happy is the man who has filled his
quiver with them. They will never be put to shame
when they speak with their enemies at the city
gate.*
    Psalm 127:3–5

Wives, submit to your husbands as to the Lord, because the husband is the head of the wife as Christ is the head of the church. He is the Savior of the body. Now as the church submits to Christ, so also wives are to submit to their husbands in everything. Husbands, love your wives, just as Christ loved the church and gave himself for her to make her holy, cleansing her with the washing of water by the word. He did this to present the church to himself in splendor, without spot or wrinkle or anything like that, but holy and blameless. In the same way, husbands are to love their wives as their own bodies. He who loves his wife loves himself.

Ephesians 5:22–28

Fathers, don't stir up anger in your children, but bring them up in the training and instruction of the Lord.

Ephesians 6:4

Father, thank You for the blessing You have given me of my family. I know I sometimes take them for granted and do not treat them as well as I should. I ask forgiveness for these transgressions against them. Please help keep me accountable for my actions towards my family. Help me to see and meet their needs. Bless them and keep them safe. Amen

Fear comes in many forms; fear of the unknown, of the impossible, of broken trust. Any of these fears can be all consuming. But we have an almighty God who loves us and cares for us at all times. We have a powerful God who is strong through all things. We have an omnipresent God who never leaves us alone, and a God who is greater than any of our fears. With God on our side, there is nothing to fear, and nothing to stand in our way.

Haven't I commanded you: be strong and
courageous? Do not be afraid or discouraged, for the
LORD your God is with you wherever you go.
   Joshua 1:9

———

When I am afraid, I will trust in you.
   Psalm 56:3

———

You did not receive a spirit of slavery to fall
back into fear. Instead, you received the Spirit of
adoption, by whom we cry out, "Abba, Father!"
   Romans 8:15

For God has not given us a spirit of fear, but one of power, love, and sound judgment.

   2 Timothy 1:7

———

Humble yourselves, therefore, under the mighty hand of God, so that he may exalt you at the proper time, casting all your cares on him, because he cares about you.

   1 Peter 5:6–7

Abba, Father, I cry out to You for Your protection and comfort. I'm overwhelmed with fear. Fear of the future, and the unknown. I know that my fear stems from distrust, and that if I truly trusted You the way I say I do, then I would not have any fear. Thank You for Your faithful love and comfort. Continue to shelter me when I feel afraid. Amen

Friendship is not usually something that just knocks on your front door and stays forever. It needs to be invited, fostered, cared for, and encouraged. It grows and changes throughout it's life. Precious are the friends, neighbors, and colleagues in our lives who faithfully stand by us through joys and sorrows, victories and failures, gains and loss. Find a way today to show the people in your life how much their friendship means to you.

Iron sharpens iron, and one person sharpens another.

    Proverbs 27:17

———

Two are better than one because they have a good reward for their efforts. For if either falls, his companion can lift him up; but pity the one who falls without another to lift him up.

    Ecclesiastes 4:9–10

———

Dear friends, let us love one another, because love is from God, and everyone who loves has been born of God and knows God.

    1 John 4:7

"No one has greater love than this: to lay down his life for his friends. You are my friends if you do what I command you. I do not call you servants anymore, because a servant doesn't know what his master is doing. I have called you friends, because I have made known to you everything I have heard from my Father."

John 15:13–15

———

Therefore encourage one another and build each other up as you are already doing.

1 Thessalonians 5:11

Lord Jesus, who called His disciples friends, thank You for demonstrating God's love for us and how best to love one another. Help me to be intentional in my relationships and to grow lifelong friendships. I thank You so much for the friends that You have placed in life, and I pray that You allow me to be a blessing to them as well. Amen

Impulsive behavior is what flows out of your heart without thought or reflection. The feeling that most reliably follows an impulsive word or action is regret, because our hearts are full of sinful desires. Choose instead to be patient and deliberate. Fill yourself with wisdom, so that when an impulsive decision is needed, what flows out instinctively is God's Word and not your own.

Discretion will watch over you, and understanding will guard you. It will rescue you from the way of evil—from anyone who says perverse things,
Proverbs 2:11–12

———

So if you have been raised with Christ, seek the things above, where Christ is, seated at the right hand of God. Set your minds on things above, not on earthly things.
Colossians 3:1–2

For we all stumble in many ways. If anyone does not stumble in what he says, he is mature, able also to control the whole body.

   James 3:2

———

Watch yourselves so you don't lose what we have worked for, but that you may receive a full reward. Anyone who does not remain in Christ's teaching but goes beyond it does not have God. The one who remains in that teaching, this one has both the Father and the Son.

   2 John 8–9

Lord God, when I am living in the urgent, my heart turns back to my sinful ways. I do the things I don't want to do, and I don't do the things I want to do. Father, I need Your help to cut away my impulsive behavior. Fill me with Your wisdom, so that I am protected from my own sinful desires. Control my words and actions, that I may not sin against You. Amen

You may have a wealth of knowledge and experience, but the deepest knowledge is awe and reverence for the Creator. God has created you with a mind capable of learning incredible things. Never take that for granted and look for opportunities daily to grow your knowledge. You never know how God will choose to use what you have learned.

For wisdom will enter your heart, and knowledge will delight you.

   Proverbs 2:10

———

For this reason also, since the day we heard this, we haven't stopped praying for you. We are asking that you may be filled with the knowledge of his will in all wisdom and spiritual understanding, so that you may walk worthy of the Lord, fully pleasing to him: bearing fruit in every good work and growing in the knowledge of God, being strengthened with all power, according to his glorious might, so that you may have great endurance and patience, joyfully giving thanks to the Father, who has enabled you to share in the saints' inheritance in the light.

   Colossians 1:9–12

The mind of the discerning acquires knowledge,
and the ear of the wise seeks it.

    Proverbs 18:15

———

For the earth will be filled with the knowledge of
the LORD's *glory, as the water covers the sea.*

    Habakkuk 2:14

———

We know that "we all have knowledge." Knowledge
puffs up, but love builds up. If anyone thinks he
knows anything, he does not yet know it as he
ought to know it. But if anyone loves God, he is
known by him.

    1 Corinthians 8:1–3

Lord, give me a desire to learn. Give me opportunities to grow in knowledge on topics that I can use to help Your Church while we are still on Earth. May your Spirit teach me Your Word and guide me in Your perfect ways, that I may be filled with the ultimate knowledge that leads to true wisdom. Amen

Work of all kinds is a gift from God to provide us with not only a living, but also a sense of purpose and service to others. When change happens it is easy to want to take a step back, and maybe even a break, but this is the time to press in and serve God with a greater determination than ever. Idle hands are the devil's playground, so never let sin catch you bored.

The slacker craves, yet has nothing, but the diligent is fully satisfied.

Proverbs 13:4

Whatever you do, do it from the heart, as something done for the Lord and not for people, knowing that you will receive the reward of an inheritance from the Lord. You serve the Lord Christ.

Colossians 3:23–24

The one who is lazy in his work is brother to a vandal.

   Proverbs 18:9

———

In fact, when we were with you, this is what we commanded you: "If anyone isn't willing to work, he should not eat."

   2 Thessalonians 3:10

Lord, when I'm feeling weary and tired, please strengthen me with the power of Your Holy Spirit. Father, fill my schedule that I may work hard for Your will and not be left with any opportunity to sin. Amen

Even surrounded by people, it is easy to feel alone. Thanks to social media, and the fast pace of modern life, many of us are left feeling isolated—but thanks to God's faithful presence and our community of believers, we never have to be alone. Jesus will never leave you or cancel plans. He is always available for you when you need Him. When you are lost in your grief, Jesus is right next to you ready to sit with you as long as you need and pull you up when you are ready.

"My presence will go with you, and I will give you rest."

    Exodus 33:14

———

The LORD is the one who will go before you. He will be with you; he will not leave you or abandon you. Do not be afraid or discouraged.

    Deuteronomy 31:8

———

God provides homes for those who are deserted. He leads out the prisoners to prosperity, but the rebellious live in a scorched land.

    Psalm 68:6

He heals the brokenhearted and bandages their wounds.

   Psalm 147:3

———

Blessed be the God and Father of our Lord Jesus Christ, the Father of mercies and the God of all comfort. He comforts us in all our affliction, so that we may be able to comfort those who are in any kind of affliction, through the comfort we ourselves receive from God.

   2 Corinthians 1:3–4

Father of mercies, please comfort me in these times of loneliness so that I may be a comfort to others. Remind me that even in my deepest despair, no matter where I am, You are with me. Thank You for being a constant reminder that I am never alone. Continue to hold me in Your arms, and help me to be a shoulder for others to help them know that I am here for them. Amen

While other people can only see our actions, God can look at our hearts and see the motives behind what we do. Rather than self-seeking or people-pleasing, we should endeavor to do all things through genuine love for God and others. But that can be harder than it sounds. Look at your full schedule of activities and examine your true motivations for each item. Are they ultimately for you, for others, or for God's glory? Use these verses to remind yourself of the importance of what is in your heart.

But the LORD said to Samuel, "Do not look at his appearance or his stature because I have rejected him. Humans do not see what the LORD sees, for humans see what is visible, but the LORD sees the heart."

1 Samuel 16:7

———

Instead, just as we have been approved by God to be entrusted with the gospel, so we speak, not to please people, but rather God, who examines our hearts.

1 Thessalonians 2:4

All a person's ways seem right to him, but the LORD
weighs hearts.

Proverbs 21:2

———

*For am I now trying to persuade people, or God? Or
am I striving to please people? If I were still trying
to please people, I would not be a servant of Christ.*

Galatians 1:10

———

*Do nothing out of selfish ambition or conceit, but
in humility consider others as more important than
yourselves.*

Philippians 2:3

Lord, please weigh my heart and my reasons for doing the things I do, and reveal to me any motives that don't glorify You. Help me to pull out those motives and change them. Give me a genuine love for the people around me, and move my heart to be so focused on You that everything I do is glorifying to Your name. Amen

The liveliness of children or the demands of the workplace can rattle your nerves, but take care to avoid making wrong choices or damaging your relationships. Remember the amount of patience that God has given you in your life, and pass it on to the people around you. Not one of us is perfect, and we all need grace and time to find the right path.

The end of a matter is better than its beginning; a patient spirit is better than a proud spirit.

    Ecclesiastes 7:8

————

Now if we hope for what we do not see, we eagerly wait for it with patience.

    Romans 8:25

————

My dear brothers and sisters, understand this: Everyone should be quick to listen, slow to speak, and slow to anger, for human anger does not accomplish God's righteousness.

    James 1:19–20

Therefore, brothers and sisters, be patient until the Lord's coming. See how the farmer waits for the precious fruit of the earth and is patient with it until it receives the early and the late rains. You also must be patient. Strengthen your hearts, because the Lord's coming is near.

James 5:7–8

———

The Lord does not delay his promise, as some understand delay, but is patient with you, not wanting any to perish but all to come to repentance.

2 Peter 3:9

Heavenly Father, You are patient and slow to anger—please help me be still and wait patiently for You. When I start to lose my way and my temper, give me Your calming touch, and help me to take a step back and remember what is really important. Thank You for the strength that You lend to me when I do not have enough for myself. Amen

No matter what trial you face or how exhausted you may feel, remember that the Lord upholds you and strengthens you at all times. This change may seem like it has been long coming, or lasted far longer than it should have. Ultimately this is the blink of an eye in eternity, and you must persevere until you are by Jesus' side.

And not only that, but we also rejoice in our
afflictions, because we know that affliction
produces endurance, endurance produces proven
character, and proven character produces hope. This
hope will not disappoint us, because God's love
has been poured out in our hearts through the Holy
Spirit who was given to us.

   Romans 5:3–5

———

Therefore, since we also have such a large cloud of
witnesses surrounding us, let us lay aside every
hindrance and the sin that so easily ensnares us.
Let us run with endurance the race that lies before
us, keeping our eyes on Jesus, the source and
perfecter of our faith. For the joy that lay before
him, he endured the cross, despising the shame,
and sat down at the right hand of the throne of God.

   Hebrews 12:1–2

Consider it a great joy, my brothers and sisters, whenever you experience various trials, because you know that the testing of your faith produces endurance. And let endurance have its full effect, so that you may be mature and complete, lacking nothing.

James 1:2–4

———

Blessed is the one who endures trials, because when he has stood the test he will receive the crown of life that God has promised to those who love him.

James 1:12

Dear Jesus, help me fix my eyes on You that Your Spirit may strengthen my heart and will to persevere. Lord, I know that I am easy to stray and quick to forget, but my desire is to run the good race and finish strong at Your side. Guide my steps that I may persevere to the end. Amen

In the same way that our friendships and relationships with people need communication to be strengthened, so does our relationship with God. He has blessed us with the ability to speak to Him at all times, whenever we need Him. Especially when we are lost in grief, the best gift is dedicated time with our Creator. No matter how we come to the Lord, whether to present our requests or to sit silently in His presence, we can trust that He hears us.

"Whenever you pray, you must not be like the hypocrites, because they love to pray standing in the synagogues and on the street corners to be seen by people. . . . But when you pray, go into your private room, shut your door, and pray to your Father who is in secret. And your Father who sees in secret will reward you. When you pray, don't babble like the Gentiles, since they imagine they'll be heard for their many words. . . .

"Therefore, you should pray like this: Our Father in heaven, your name be honored as holy. Your kingdom come. Your will be done on earth as it is in heaven. Give us today our daily bread. And forgive us our debts, as we also have forgiven our debtors. And do not bring us into temptation, but deliver us from the evil one.

"For if you forgive others their offenses, your heavenly Father will forgive you as well. But if you don't forgive others, your Father will not forgive your offenses."

Matthew 6:5–15

*"If you remain in me and my words remain in you,
ask whatever you want and it will be done for you."*

    John 15:7

———

*In the same way the Spirit also helps us in our
weakness, because we do not know what to pray for
as we should, but the Spirit himself intercedes for
us with unspoken groanings.*

    Romans 8:26

———

*Don't worry about anything, but in everything,
through prayer and petition with thanksgiving,
present your requests to God.*

    Philippians 4:6

Lord Jesus, just as You taught Your followers how to pray, instill in me a deep desire to seek Your presence. Send reminders into my life of my need to spend time with You. Help me to remember to not only speak in my prayers, but to sit and listen to what You have to say to me. Give me rest in Your presence that my spirit may be healed. Amen

Pride comes in many shapes and sizes. Arrogance tells us we are better than others, low self-esteem tells us we are worse, and praise makes us feel important, but they are all signs of pride, because they all put the focus on ourselves. Though we may be blessed with wisdom, success, and happy relationships, we can avoid pride by remembering that all good things are ours by the grace of God.

When arrogance comes, disgrace follows, but with humility comes wisdom.

    Proverbs 11:2

———

Everyone with a proud heart is detestable to the LORD; be assured, he will not go unpunished.

    Proverbs 16:5

———

A person's pride will humble him, but a humble spirit will gain honor.

    Proverbs 29:23

*Live in harmony with one another. Do not be proud;
instead, associate with the humble. Do not be wise
in your own estimation.*

Romans 12:16

———

*For if anyone considers himself to be something
when he is nothing, he deceives himself.*

Galatians 6:3

Father God, please forgive the ways I puff myself up rather than humble myself under Your loving hand. Help me to forget about myself, and keep my eyes on You. When I fall into a trap of pride, pull me to repentance that I may not continue to sin against You. I know that any good I am capable of is only because of You. Amen

Our deepest purpose is not in what we do but in who we are—people who love, honor, and praise the only One who is worthy. It is the purpose that each of us was created for—to glorify God.

When all has been heard, the conclusion of the matter is this: fear God and keep his commands, because this is for all humanity.

Ecclesiastes 12:13

―――

But I consider my life of no value to myself; my purpose is to finish my course and the ministry I received from the Lord Jesus, to testify to the gospel of God's grace.

Acts 20:24

"My Father is glorified by this: that you produce much fruit and prove to be my disciples."

    John 15:8

———

He has saved us and called us with a holy calling, not according to our works, but according to his own purpose and grace, which was given to us in Christ Jesus before time began.

    2 Timothy 1:9

———

Sing to him; sing praise to him; tell about all his wondrous works! Honor his holy name; let the hearts of those who seek the LORD rejoice.

    1 Chronicles 16:9–10

Lord Jesus, may each day offer me opportunities to live out my true purpose by loving and serving You and those around me who were created in Your image. Guide my steps down the path You have created for me, that I may glorify You in all that I do. Amen

We often think of self-control in terms of moral behavior, but consider also the importance of holding our tongues—a person's speech should be measured and gracious. When we are in the midst of change, it is easy to become lost in the chaos of the unknown and forget about the boundaries and wisdom that you have been blessed with. Hold fast to the truth of Scripture, so that no matter how you are blown about, you will always stay true to the Holy Scriptures.

A person who does not control his temper is like a city whose wall is broken down.

Proverbs 25:28

———

No temptation has come upon you except what is common to humanity. But God is faithful; he will not allow you to be tempted beyond what you are able, but with the temptation he will also provide a way out so that you may be able to bear it.

1 Corinthians 10:13

Finally brothers and sisters, whatever is true, whatever is honorable, whatever is just, whatever is pure, whatever is lovely, whatever is commendable—if there is any moral excellence and if there is anything praiseworthy—dwell on these things.

   Philippians 4:8

———

Be sober-minded, be alert. Your adversary the devil is prowling around like a roaring lion, looking for anyone he can devour.

   1 Peter 5:8

Lord God, when I struggle with temptation or am quick to anger, please renew Your gentle Spirit within me. Do not allow me to become overwhelmed by the chaos of this world, but be at peace in Your plan. Place in me the patience to seek out wisdom over impulse. Amen

In an unstable world, with change around every corner, only God is a reliable foundation. No matter what change you are going through, if you have built your life around God, you will not fall. With this everlasting stability, feel the freedom to change, knowing that you will always have your most important constant.

*I always let the L*ORD* guide me. Because he is at my right hand, I will not be shaken.*

Psalm 16:8

———

He brought me up from a desolate pit, out of the muddy clay, and set my feet on a rock, making my steps secure.

Psalm 40:2

The person who trusts in the Lord, *whose confidence indeed is the* Lord, *is blessed. He will be like a tree planted by water: it sends its roots out toward a stream, it doesn't fear when heat comes, and its foliage remains green. It will not worry in a year of drought or cease producing fruit.*

Jeremiah 17:7–8

———

Therefore, since we are receiving a kingdom that cannot be shaken, let us be thankful. By it, we may serve God acceptably, with reverence and awe, for our God is a consuming fire.

Hebrews 12:28–29

Father, sometimes I feel like I am wandering through a desert, making changes that are only going to get me more lost. Send me daily reminders of Your steadfast stability. Lord, thank You for being my constant companion through the changes of life. I lay myself fully into Your hands, because I know You are worthy of all trust. Amen

Chronic stress is quickly becoming a national crisis that threatens our health—but God is our ever-present helper in times of trouble. Lay your burdens at His feet, and do not allow yourself to become overwhelmed with the temporary problems of this world. Cast your burdens on Him, and He will carry you through this time of stress.

Cast your burden on the LORD, and he will sustain you; he will never allow the righteous to be shaken.

Psalm 55:22

————

Commit your activities to the LORD, and your plans will be established.

Proverbs 16:3

————

"For I am the LORD your God, who holds your right hand, who says to you, 'Do not fear, I will help you.'"

Isaiah 41:13

"*Come to me, all of you who are weary and burdened, and I will give you rest. Take up my yoke and learn from me, because I am lowly and humble in heart, and you will find rest for your souls. For my yoke is easy and my burden is light.*"

Matthew 11:28–30

———

I am able to do all things through him who strengthens me.

Philippians 4:13

Dear God, please fill me and strengthen me with Your Spirit when I feel overwhelmed, exhausted, and uncertain. Give me peace during the stress. Remind me daily of what You have trusted me to handle, and what I need to lay down at Your feet. Help me to trust You and to know that nothing I do can ever get in the way of Your plan. Amen

When you are in a pit of grief, it can be difficult to find things to be grateful for. But the more we practice gratitude and thanksgiving, the more abundance and goodness we recognize all around us. Even on your lowest day, find ways to thank God.

Every good and perfect gift is from above, coming down from the Father of lights, who does not change like shifting shadows.

James 1:17

———

For we know that the one who raised the Lord Jesus will also raise us with Jesus and present us with you. Indeed, everything is for your benefit so that, as grace extends through more and more people, it may cause thanksgiving to increase to the glory of God.

2 Corinthians 4:14–16

Give thanks to the LORD, for he is good; his faithful love endures forever.

Psalm 118:1

———

Let the word of Christ dwell richly among you, in all wisdom teaching and admonishing one another through psalms, hymns, and spiritual songs, singing to God with gratitude in your hearts.

Colossians 3:16

———

Rejoice always, pray constantly, give thanks in everything; for this is God's will for you in Christ Jesus.

1 Thessalonians 5:16–18

Father, I praise You and thank You for every good and perfect gift You have given. I thank You for Your constant comfort and guiding light. Help me to never lose sight of Your blessings. Sooth my aching soul and show me how to glorify You through my suffering. Amen

Trust is not an easy thing to give away. Everyone has had a time when their trust has been given to a friend, only to be betrayed. But God is not a fallible human. To trust the Lord is to believe what He has said about Himself: He is good, faithful, and sovereign. He is always worthy and deserving of our trust.

The person who trusts in the LORD, whose confidence indeed is the LORD, is blessed. He will be like a tree planted by water: it sends its roots out toward a stream, it doesn't fear when heat comes, and its foliage remains green. It will not worry in a year of drought or cease producing fruit.

   Jeremiah 17:7–8

———

I will be with you when you pass through the waters, and when you pass through the rivers, they will not overwhelm you. You will not be scorched when you walk through the fire, and the flame will not burn you.

   Isaiah 43:2

*Wait for the L*ORD*; be strong, and let your heart be courageous. Wait for the L*ORD*.*
Psalm 27:14

————

And my God will supply all your needs according to his riches in glory in Christ Jesus.
Philippians 4:19

————

This is the confidence we have before him: If we ask anything according to his will, he hears us.
1 John 5:14

Dear God, thank You for working all things together for the good of those who love You and are called according to Your purpose. Thank You for being worthy of my trust and forgiving me when I question You. I praise Your matchless faithfulness. Help my disbelief. Amen

Though we may have advanced degrees and years of experience, this without the Spirit gives us only knowledge and not true wisdom with what to do with the information. The Holy Spirit, who helps us discern what is true, good, and right, will bless you with wisdom when you seek Him out. Study the Scriptures, so that when you are in times of trial, wisdom pours out of your heart.

Teach us to number our days carefully so that we may develop wisdom in our hearts.

    Psalm 90:12

———

Do not be conformed to this age, but be transformed by the renewing of your mind, so that you may discern what is the good, pleasing, and perfect will of God.

    Romans 12:2

Yet to those who are called, both Jews and Greeks, Christ is the power of God and the wisdom of God, because God's foolishness is wiser than human wisdom, and God's weakness is stronger than human strength.

  1 Corinthians 1:24–25

———

Now if any of you lacks wisdom, he should ask God—who gives to all generously and ungrudgingly—and it will be given to him.

  James 1:5

Heavenly Father, who gives generously and freely, please fill me with Your wisdom for how to be righteous. Guide my steps, and transform my mind, that I may see the world with Your eyes and truly understand what is at stake behind sinful decisions. Father, teach me to be wise that I may not stray from Your side. Amen

Worry is false and useless fear—it's imagining and anticipating what might happen but probably won't. What can you change by worrying about it? Nothing. What can you fix by thinking about everything that could go wrong? Nothing. Instead, spend your time focused on today. On what you can do, on what you know to be truth, and leave the rest to God.

"Therefore I tell you: Don't worry about your life, what you will eat or what you will drink; or about your body, what you will wear. Isn't life more than food and the body more than clothing? Consider the birds of the sky: They don't sow or reap or gather into barns, yet your heavenly Father feeds them. Aren't you worth more than they? Can any of you add one moment to his life-span by worrying?"

 Matthew 6:25–27

———

We know that all things work together for the good of those who love God, who are called according to his purpose.

 Romans 8:28

The Lord answered her, "Martha, Martha, you are worried and upset about many things, but one thing is necessary. Mary has made the right choice, and it will not be taken away from her."

   Luke 10:41–42

———

Don't worry about anything, but in everything, through prayer and petition with thanksgiving, present your requests to God. And the peace of God, which surpasses all understanding, will guard your hearts and minds in Christ Jesus.

   Philippians 4:6–7

Lord Jesus, I am often worried about many things. I worry about tomorrow, about my family, about what friends are really thinking, about health, about clothes, about money, and about countless other meaningless things. Jesus, I know that my worry will do nothing; but the thoughts are rooted in my mind, and I know I cannot remove them without Your help. Remind me of Your provision. Show me ways to let go of my worry. Please grant me a heart like Mary, who rested at Your feet. Amen

VERSE INDEX